Antistress Therapy: The Artful Path

101 mandalas and inspirations from the fine arts to ensure your well-being

Tom eMusic — Nanook Books

Chief Editor
Tamara Fonteyn

Illustrations
Blake Bendezar, Sylvie Malon

Cover Art
Arthur Friday

Artistic Director
Pauline Marie, Madeleine Rook

Iconography
Katarzyna Alonso, Pauline Marie

Proofreaders
Dena Angevin, Ben Torrent

ISBN 978-1-62321-110-3

www.tomemusic.com
www.nanookbooks.com

Table of Contents

The Sacred Art of Tibet

The art of constructing mandalas, which are detailed visualizations of Buddhist deities and symbolic objects arranged in a precise order, appeared in Tibet approximately 2,000 years ago. A 'mandala' is a Sanskrit word which signifies the form and concept of centrality as well as, by extension, the periphery and whatever surrounds it. Mandalas typically represent within their inner circle a deity, which is surrounded by its sacred entourage. The palace and its walls, doors, floors and the deities who inhabit it constitute the graphic elements of mandalas. These complex representations of energies and the operation of the invisible universe are a support for meditation.

Buddhist monks created mandalas in the sand, which aided them in gaining self-knowledge and spiritual development. As a symbolic representation of the universe, the mandala guides the practitioner towards inner unity and aids in establishing natural links with others and the surrounding world. Meditation on the mandala is accompanied by an entire liturgy, which includes rituals or the repetition of mantras. At the conclusion of the liturgy, the mandala is designed to symbolize the transience of life.

Ancient Egyptian Art

Egyptian art is one of the most beautiful and original artistic phenomena in human history. It had a considerable influence over the art of other ancient civilizations as well as more recent forms of art as in the case of Empire style.

Egyptian art was subordinated to religion. Although the themes of paintings varied, the religious and funerary scenes that enriched numerous hieroglyphic inscriptions can no doubt be considered the most characteristic. The Egyptians believed that the human soul could be reborn several times. With great care, they prepared the graves to ensure a peaceful passage to the new lives awaiting the dead. The paintings that decorated the walls of these tombs played a major role during this passage.

Paints were applied directly onto the construction materials. The images and also the colors used had each their symbolic meaning. For example, white represented deliverance from the evil power of demons; red symbolized life and yellow eternity.

In Egyptian art, human beings were depicted in a very unique fashion. The head, legs and hands were painted in profile, while the eyes, arms and chest faced viewers.

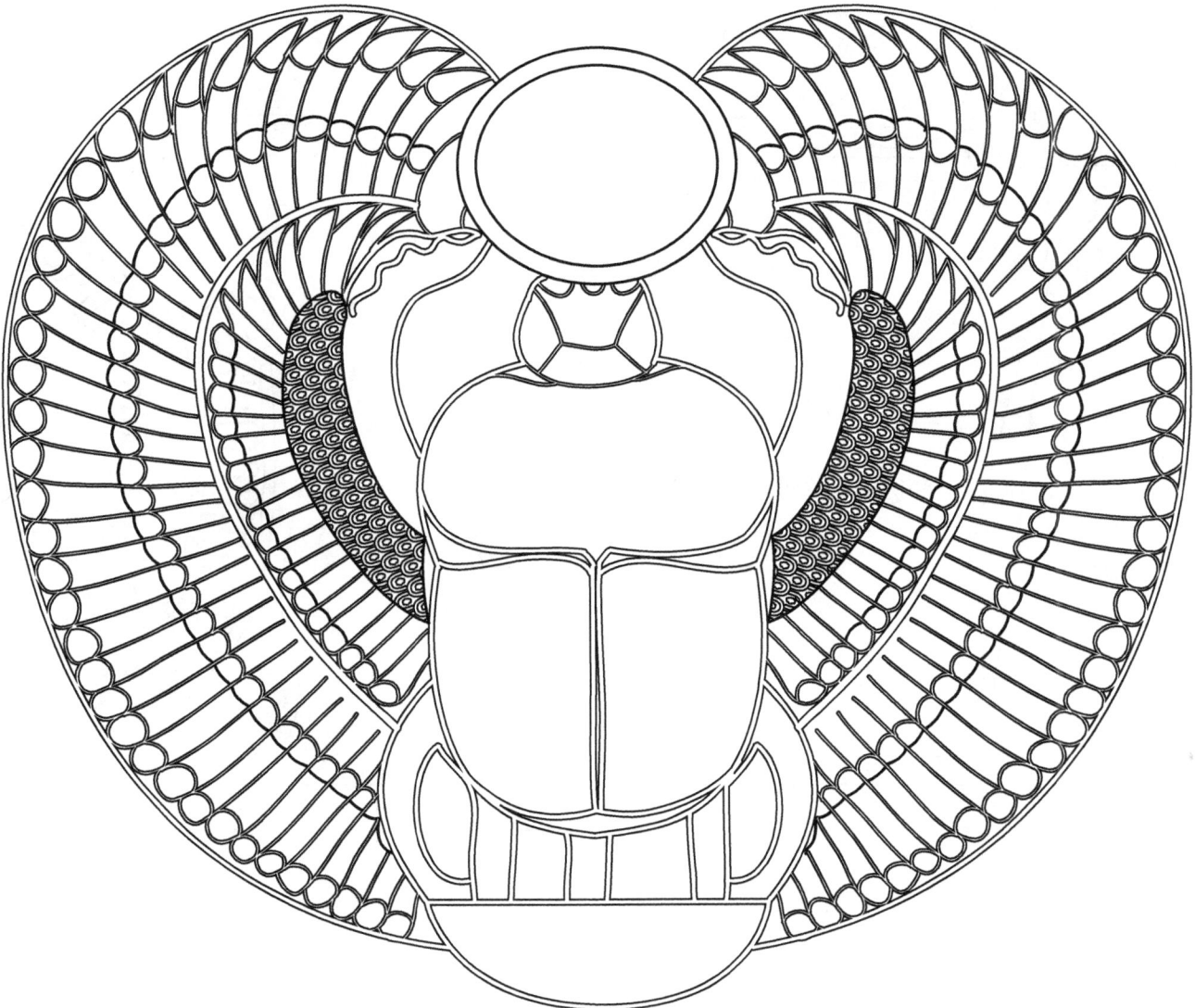

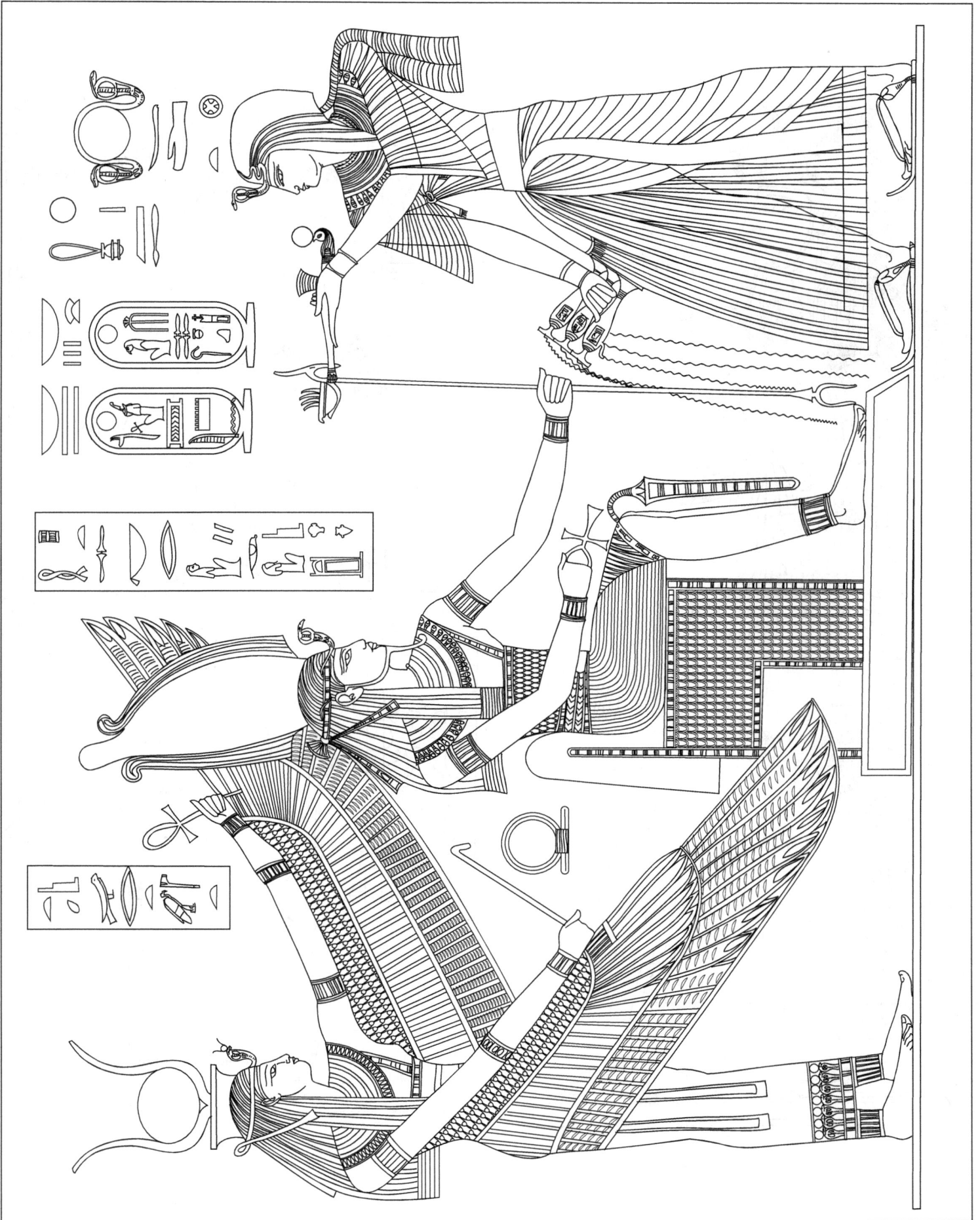

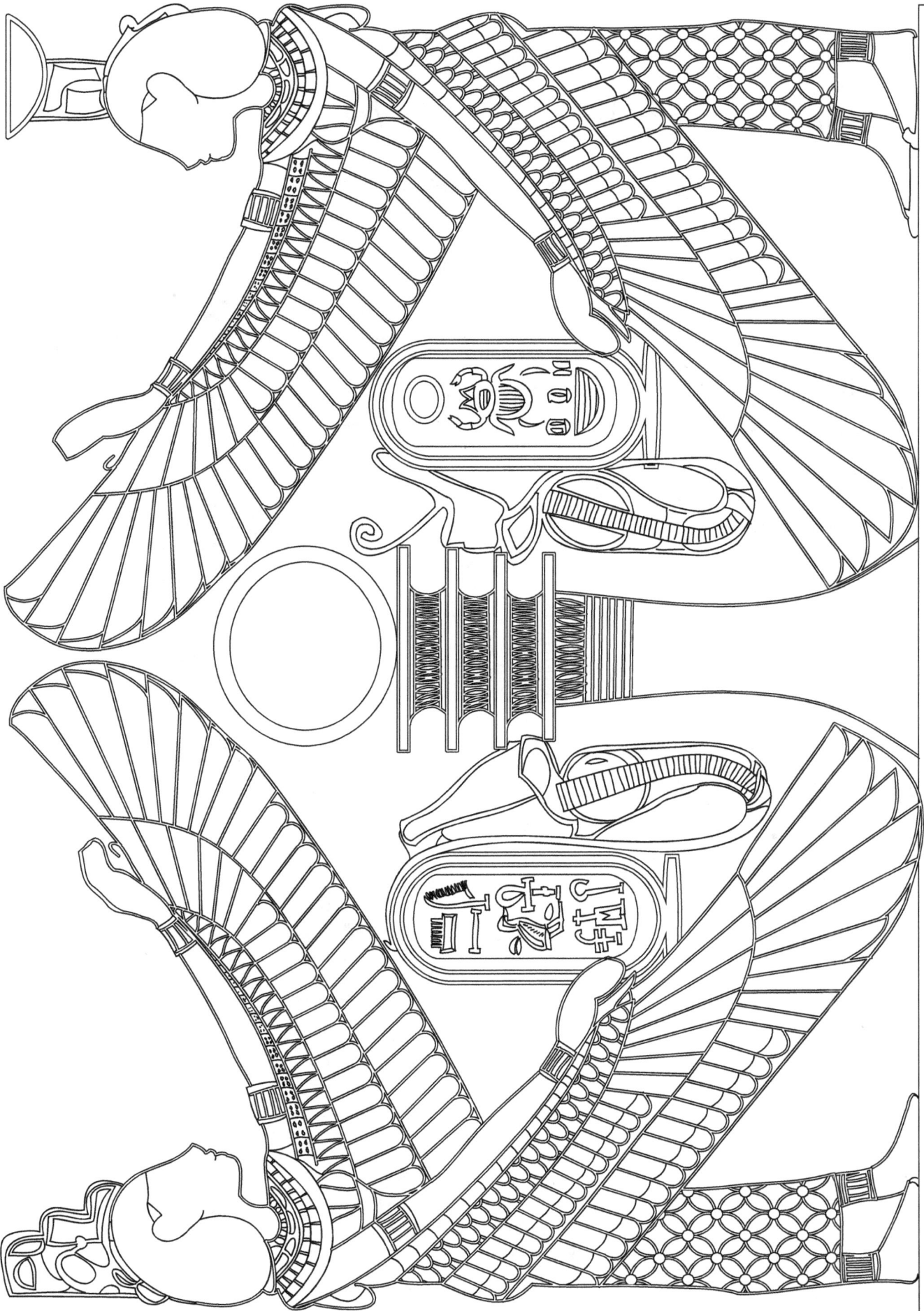

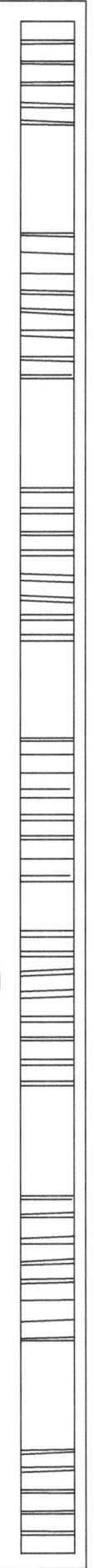

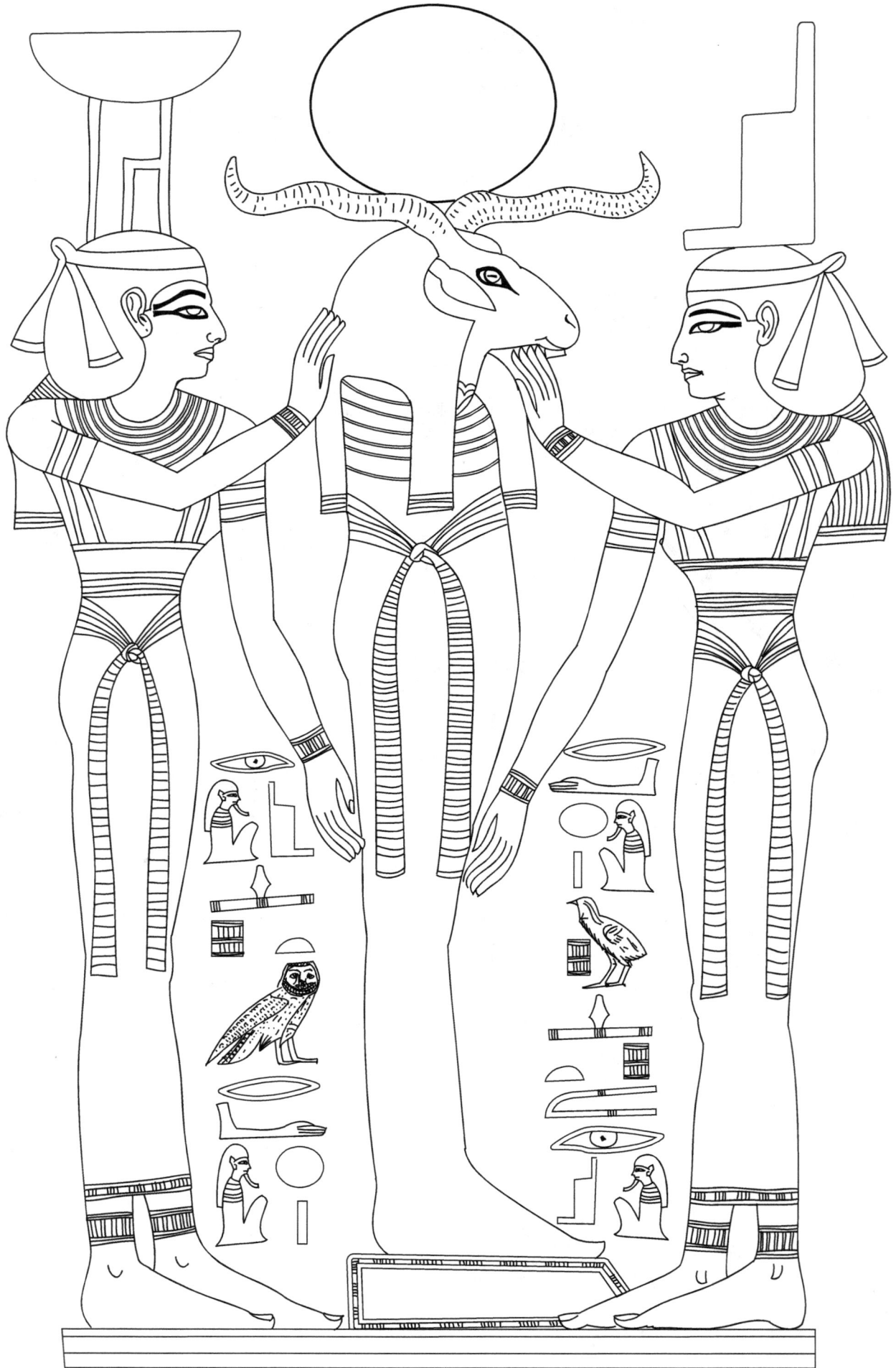

Persian Rugs

The first Persian rugs were woven at least 2,500 years ago. Common practice was to place them on the floor to protect people from the cold and humidity. For centuries, the production of rugs was ensured by nomadic tribes from the Orient, a secret craft passed on from generation to generation and jealously guarded. The techniques of rug weaving experienced incredible development in ancient Persia. Little by little the production of these works was organized into a veritable industry. Decorated with geometric forms, animal figures and floral motives, rugs were woven from wool, cotton and silk, and sometimes even gold and silver. As the Persian symbol of life, the image of a rose was often reproduced.

From the 13th century, these products of great beauty and value were imported to Europe where they became symbols of wealth and prestige. The art of weaving reached its peak of refinement under the Safavid dynasty that ruled Iran in the 16th and 17th centuries.

The Art of Islam

Despite the great diversity due to the geographical reach of Islamic civilization, the pictorial art of Islam offers a kind of stylistic unity with respect to its attention to the decorative element and in particular, decorative vegetation, geometry and calligraphy. One other characteristic ubiquitous in Islamic art is the use of vivid colors such as gold, red, violet, green and brown.

Islamic art is typically divided into at least two groups, one which includes banned representations of living creatures and another that features figurative representations. On one hand, Islam is part of the aniconic tradition. Artworks consist only of geometric motives, arabesques or calligraphic elements. The decorations that cover mosques or sacred books reflect the refinement and elegance of this art, which approaches the abstract.

On the other, the interpretation of sacred Islamic texts is not immune to change. In different times and places, art in the lands of Islam also gave rise to animal and human figures, most notably featured in secular architecture, ceramics, textiles and painting.

Stained-Glass Windows

The stained-glass window appeared in medieval architecture around the 10th century. From that time, its artistry and technical form excelled, as demonstrated by the oldest pieces that have been preserved such as the Head of Christ of Wissembourg. During the 13th century, the stained-glass window became the principal form of monumental painting. Its peak is closely associated with the construction of Gothic cathedrals in Europe.

Cathedral windows expressed the Christian symbolism of light. When sunlight shines through the windows, it is symbolically transfigured into divine light. Windows were used as illustration of the life of Christ or those of the saints. They also taught believers about the Old and New Testaments.

Rosettes represent the most perfect work of medieval artists. The scenes that are represented seem to merge into a single abstract explosion of colors and light in the image of the glory of God. In France, these masterpieces of the art of stained glass can be admired in the cathedrals of Chartres, Le Mans, Poitiers and Paris.

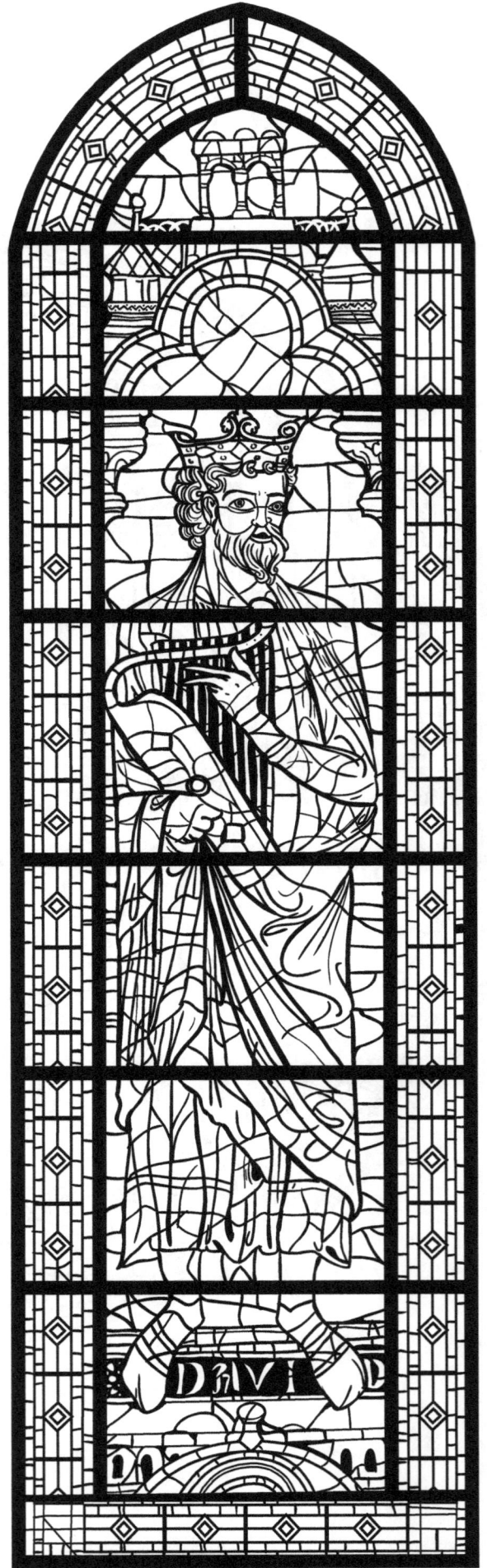

17ᵗʰ and 18ᵗʰ Century Marquetry Art

Inlay is the art of decorating furniture and small objects of daily use by embedding patterns (images) made with contrasting materials such as wood, stone or metal. This technique has existed around the world since ancient times but experienced the most development during the Renaissance and Baroque periods and evolved into the art of marquetry.

At the end of the 16ᵗʰ century, Italian artists, inspired by the mosaics of the Roman Empire, created a new style of furniture decoration called 'Pietra dura' or 'Florentine mosaic'. Under the leadership of Cardinal Ferdinando I de Medici at the beginning of the 17ᵗʰ century, in Florence and Rome appeared the first workshops which produced quality furniture adorned with mosaics of marble and other stones such as agate and lapis lazuli. This was the period when majestic accent tables were designed and drawn by Jacopo Ligozzi. Colored patterns representing flowers, fruit and birds were featured on the surface of black Flemish marble using the Florentine inlay technique.

In France, under the reign of Louis XIV, the most celebrated marquetry artist was André-Charles Boulle. He created luxurious royal furniture as well as furnishings for the aristocracy, ornamented with plant tendrils and arabesques using the marquetry technique. A recurring theme is presented on Boulle's furniture: a face surrounded by palms whose leaves are transformed into rays. The cabinets, tables and wardrobes created using this extraordinarily decorative technique can be admired at the Palace of Versailles, the Louvre and British museums.

Art Nouveau Painting

At the end of the 19th century, a new and extraordinary style developed in the European art world: Art Nouveau, which represented a complete break with previous trends. Its name varies from one country to another. While it is called Art Nouveau in France, the term 'Jugendstil' is used in Germany and 'Stile Floreale' in Italy.

Art nouveau takes its inspiration from, among others, Celtic and Japanese arts. Its distinctive features are luxury and decoration, abstract ornamentation as well as the use of undulating lines that are incredibly sophisticated.

At the time, Austria was the principal center for the development of Art Nouveau as well as home to two remarkable artists: Alfons Mucha (1860-1939) and Gustav Klimt (1862-1918). The Czech artist Alfons Mucha mainly created graphic representations of idealized figures of beautiful women surrounded by Byzantine, naturalist and arabesques patterns. Contrastingly, Judith II or Salomé and Portrait of Adèle Bloch-Bauer I are examples, among others, of Gustav Klimt's style, which involved female figures with realistic heads against abstract backgrounds.

F. CHAMPENOIS

IMPRIMEUR-ÉDITEUR
66. Boul.º S.ᵗ Michel.

PARIS

1898   1898

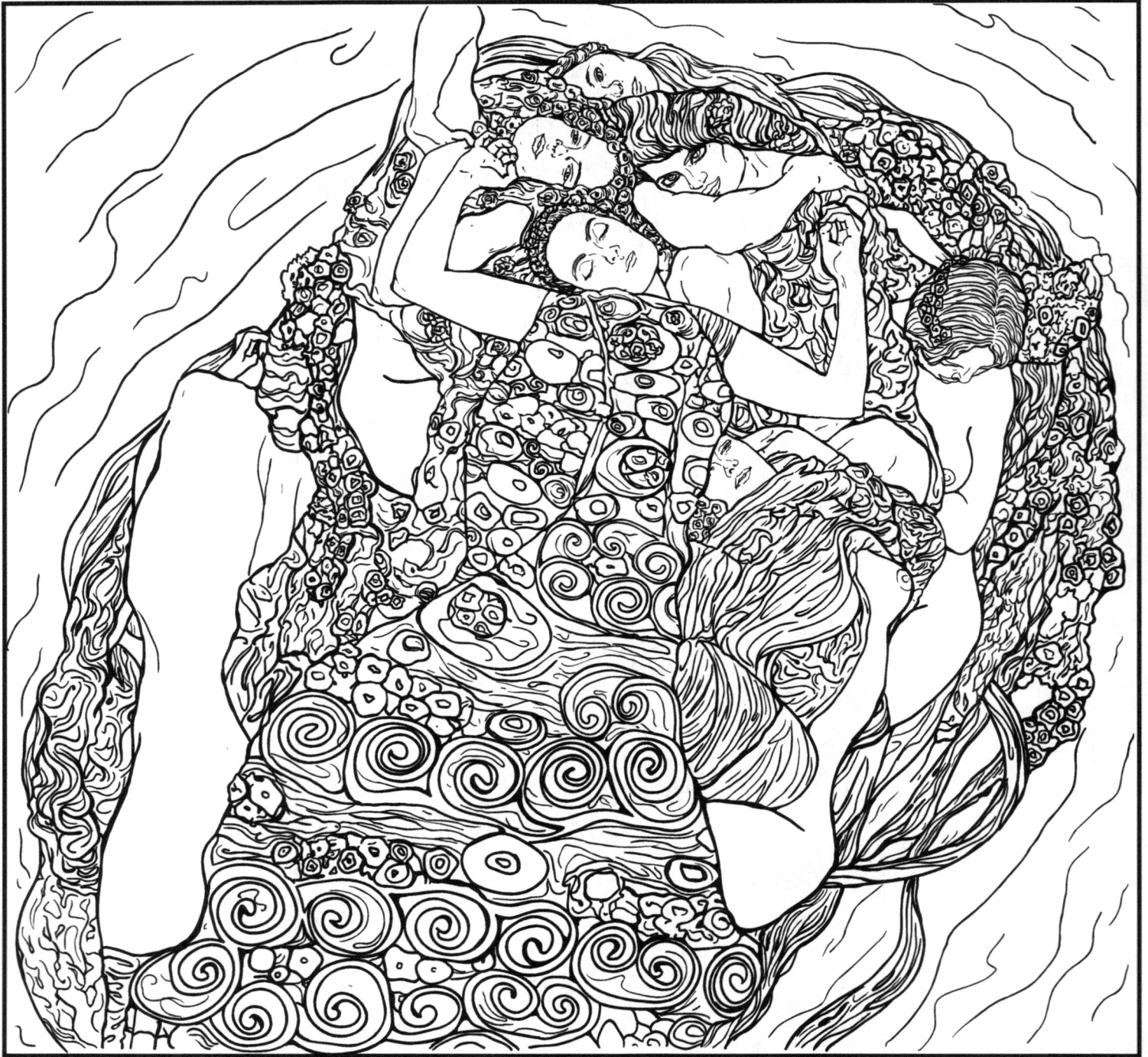

Index

All the illustrations in this book are creative interpretations of the following works of art:

www.ingramcontent.com/pod-product-compliance
Lightning Source LLC
Chambersburg PA
CBHW081239020426

42331CB00013B/3232